GREEN NATION
REVOLUTION

LAURENCE KING

Published by
Laurence King Publishing Ltd
361–373 City Road
London EC1V 1LR
United Kingdom
Tel: +44 20 7841 6900
E-mail: enquiries@laurenceking.com
www.laurenceking.com

A catalogue record for this book is available
from the British Library

ISBN: 978-1-78627-765-7

© 2019 Centauria srl – Milano
Text © Valentina Giannella and Lucia Esther Maruzzelli
Illustrations © Manuela Marazzi
Graphic design PEPE nymi
Translation by JMS Books llp
Typeset by Marie Doherty
Cover design by Florian Michelet

Printed in China

Laurence King Publishing is committed to
ethical and sustainable production. We are
proud participants in The Book Chain Project®
bookchainproject.com

BOOK CHAIN PROJECT

GREEN NATION REVOLUTION

USE YOUR FUTURE TO CHANGE THE WORLD

Valentina Giannella and Lucia Esther Maruzzelli

Illustrations by Manuela Marazzi

Laurence King Publishing

CONTENTS

For the young people of the world:
for the Green Nation.

INTRODUCTION

The last two years have played a crucial role in our understanding of climate change. The extraordinary ability of a young girl, Greta Thunberg, to publicize issues that scientists have been trying to bring to the attention of both politicians and the public, for more than thirty years, has awakened the conscience of entire generations. In particular, it has spoken to young people, who are ready to change the rules and have elected to speak one language – the language of science. Through the movements that emerged from Fridays for Future and the global Climate Strikes, their voices have united to form an umbrella entity that we have come to view as a sovereign power without borders: a Green Nation.

Who are the young citizens of this Green Nation? What do they want? Most importantly, what do they hope to achieve? This book reveals the steps that can be taken in the immediate future to shape their destiny and help make the Earth a safer place for everyone, from humans to the entire biosphere.

It follows the success of *We Are All Greta*, in which the key aspects underlying climate change were examined using findings from the most authoritative international research bodies.

Once they fully understood the situation, young people faced their first question: what now? And the answer? Plenty of action is needed in every single sector, based on proper study, inspired ideas and hard work. We dedicate *Green Nation Revolution* to this question and to those asking it.

'THE NECESSARY TRANSFORMATION OF THE GLOBAL ECONOMY NEEDS TO BE PLANNED SYSTEMATICALLY AND INCLUSIVELY. A NET-ZERO FUTURE MUST DELIVER ON ALL THE SUSTAINABLE DEVELOPMENT GOALS. AND AS WE PURSUE CLIMATE STABILITY AND RESILIENCE, WE SHOULD COMMIT TO BUILDING SOCIETIES THAT ARE FAIR AS WELL AS PROSPEROUS, BY TARGETING TODAY'S STAGGERING LEVELS OF INEQUALITY.'

DAME POLLY COURTICE, DIRECTOR OF THE UNIVERSITY OF CAMBRIDGE INSTITUTE FOR SUSTAINABLE LEADERSHIP

'THERE'S A NEW FORCE OF NATURE AT HAND, STIRRING ALL OVER THE WORLD. THEY ARE THE YOUNG PEOPLE WHOM, FRANKLY, WE HAVE FAILED. WHO ARE ANGRY, WHO ARE ORGANIZED, WHO ARE CAPABLE OF MAKING A DIFFERENCE. THEY WILL NOT BE DENIED, BECAUSE THEY ARE RIGHT. THEY ARE A MORAL ARMY. AND THE MOST IMPORTANT THING WE CAN DO FOR THEM IS TO GET THE HELL OUT OF THEIR WAY.'

HARRISON FORD, ACTOR AND CLIMATE ACTIVIST

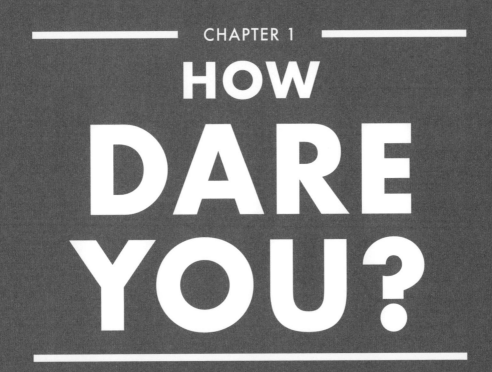

CHAPTER 1

HOW DARE YOU?

GRETA, TODAY

How dare you? **Greta Thunberg**

Her gaze is resolute, although, unusually, her voice trembles, betraying emotion unsuspected before. As she addresses the crowd gathered within the United Nations building in New York for the Climate Action Summit of 23 September 2019, Greta Thunberg is wearing her hair in one thick plait for the first time. Gone are the two girlish pigtails which, along with her yellow raincoat, had become the symbol of the first Climate Strike. She wears a pink shirt and her face is tense, her eyes fixed upon the space between the dais and the dozens of cameras lined up for the event.

'You have stolen my dreams and my childhood with your empty words. And yet, I am one of the lucky ones. People are suffering. People are dying. Entire ecosystems are collapsing. We are in the beginning of a mass extinction – and all you can talk about is money and fairy tales of eternal economic growth. How dare you?'

Greta has changed in the few short months since the Monday in August 2018 when she decided not to go to school. Seated in front of the Swedish Parliament building, she held up for the first inquisitive journalists a sign that would inspire millions of young people: *Skolstrejk för klimatet.* The seventeen-year-old who has cast a spotlight on thirty years of climate change science has matured into a global leader without a trace of indecision. She is fearless. 'How dare you?' was a warning to the planet's leaders and it is now a slogan for children around the globe.

The numbers speak for themselves: from May to December 2019, participants in the Climate Strike increased almost tenfold, from 1.4 million to more than 12 million, including the week of global strikes held in November that year.

Public squares, from New Zealand to Afghanistan, have witnessed gatherings of children who share the fears of climate scientists. Hundreds of countries, regions and cities around the world have announced a state of climate emergency and agreed to place the issue at the top of the political agenda. Dozens of teenagers have filed official reports against their leaders for failing to take the future of later generations into account, a serious violation of the

International Convention on the Rights of the Child. Even Pope Francis and Barack Obama have become Greta followers and have played host to her as she raises the alarm to governments.

The message uniting these young people is the same as the one implicitly promoted since the late 1980s by thousands of scientists working on the reports of the Intergovernmental Panel on Climate Change (IPCC): the planet is warming; human activity is causing this increase in temperature and the only way to fight it is for governments around the globe to take action on a major scale.

So, what should that action be? The starting point to understanding just what is required lies in Greta's own words: 'fairy tales of eternal economic growth'. The key to tackling climate change is economic action, and Greta and other young people are now aware of this. It is no longer enough to change your lifestyle (as millions of young people are already doing through their own climate action). The time has now come to revolutionize the way we think about the entire global economy, and to rethink the jobs of tomorrow.

And that is why we have written this book. We want to understand how we can prepare for a future that could still hold positive surprises if we go about it in the right way.

THE FIRST BIT OF GOOD NEWS

When a tree grows, it becomes taller and has more foliage (and becomes the perfect place to shelter from the sun's rays during a summer picnic). It also absorbs carbon dioxide from the air and stores it within itself. As has been pointed out by **George Monbiot** (a science popularizer and journalist for the British newspaper *The Guardian*) in the Protect, Restore and Fund campaign, a tree is a 'magic machine that sucks carbon out of the air, costs very little and builds itself'.

We have always known about the photosynthesis of chlorophyll, the process through which plants turn carbon dioxide into substances needed for growth. We were, however, unaware of the extent to which preserving and planting woodland (forestation) can help combat global warming. Forests are currently being decimated at the rate of 30 football fields per minute, but research carried out by Professor **Thomas Crowther** at Zurich's ETH university has indeed shown the extraordinary potential of the simple act of planting trees: 'We all knew that restoring forests could play a part in tackling climate change, but we didn't really know how big the impact would be. Our study shows clearly that forest restoration is the best climate-change solution available today.' As long as we stop burning fossil fuels at the same time, of course.

Where should we plant these trees? There is enough space for billions more, and there's no need to panic – it's not on land currently used for agriculture or urban development, or for cities and inhabited areas. According to the research, regions currently unused by humans and amounting to 11 percent of the Earth's entire land surface area (roughly equivalent to the territories of the United States and China combined) could support trees, plants and mangroves, or any species of vegetation compatible with local climatic conditions.

CHAPTER 2

WHEN THE GOING GETS TOUGH

THE POWER OF GRETA, FROM THE MEDIA TO THE UNITED NATIONS

As John Belushi pointed out in the cult film *Animal House*: 'When the going gets tough, the tough get going.' And, when you really start to make waves and influence public opinion, those in power are forced to sit up and take notice of you. For better or worse.

The months of strikes, meetings, speeches and interviews with Greta had gained increasing media attention for the fight against climate change, and greater access to the agendas of public administrators. In December 2019, Greta climbed to the giddy heights of the cover of *Time* magazine as their Person of the Year. 'Change is coming, whether you like it or not,' she reiterated, and many finally began to wonder if she was right. Even if they didn't have faith in her, they could believe the science to which she has given a face and a voice.

Her success has attracted the attention not only of those citizens of the world worried about the future (their own and their children's) but also of climate-change deniers of all kinds. Those who chose to ignore the scientists' call to action were now all too aware of the challenge posed by a warning from a seventeen-year-old girl in the spotlight of billions of people – including politicians' own constituents.

From the ranks of the most famous deniers, two in particular have made use of their public influence to diminish Greta's role and influence – and thereby that of science itself – after her speech at the United Nations (UN). The first was Donald Trump, president of the United States. Perhaps disconcerted by polls suggesting that Americans were becoming increasingly concerned about climate change, and after his administration withdrew the United States (one of the world's most polluting nations) from the 2015 Paris Agreement on emission reductions, Trump hurried away from the UN meeting at which Greta spoke. Shortly after her speech, he tweeted: 'She seems like a very happy young girl looking forward to a bright and wonderful future. So nice to see!' With heavy irony, Greta added this to her Twitter bio for a few hours.

Vladimir Putin, Trump's Russian counterpart, chose a rather more institutional tone to disparage her: 'No one has explained to Greta that the modern world is complex and different.' Or perhaps it is just better for them if we all think so, enabling certain leaders to continue to act in the interests of a select few, flying unchallenged in the face of science.

Greta's message is not for those who merely pay lip service to supporting her, especially public figures who have the power to change laws but fail to act decisively enough. Justin Trudeau, prime minister of Canada, knows about this all too well. Having met Greta and voiced to the whole world his admiration for her work in raising awareness, he was publicly reprimanded on social media by Greta herself for 'obviously not doing enough'.

The discreet distance that Greta has always maintained from politics of any colour is summed up in one of her pronouncements, September 2019: 'The climate and ecological crisis is beyond party politics. And our main enemy right now is not our political opponents. Our main enemy now is physics, and we cannot make "deals" with physics.'

Science, determination, deliberate use of the mainstream media and social media. No political side. The young people of this new generation are constructing an identity that adults are still struggling to get a handle on. Is this why they inspire so much fear?

SMALL LEADERS GROW

'I'm just a messenger,' Greta has said again and again. 'If everyone listened to the scientists and the facts that I constantly refer to, then no one would have to listen to me or any of the other hundreds of thousands of school children on strike for the climate across the world. Then we could all go back to school.' In no time at all, this charismatic teenage Swede has inspired other young leaders like her to create new environmentalist movements.

These include the likes of **Anna Taylor**, a nineteen-year-old Englishwoman who founded the **UK Student Climate Network** with four of her school friends; twenty-year-old **Katie Eder** of the **Future Coalition** movement; **Anuna De Wever** and **Kyra Gantois**, Flemish students whose efforts, at nineteen and twenty respectively, alone brought 35,000 people to a public square. Or fifteen-year-old **Alexandria Villaseñor**, an asthma sufferer whose life was endangered on a trip to Northern California when she breathed in the smoke from a burning forest (which had claimed the lives of almost a hundred people); she went on to found the uncompromising **School Strike 4 Climate**. As Greta says, you are never too young to make a difference.

CHAPTER 3

RIGHT HERE, RIGHT NOW

THE GENESIS OF
THE GREEN NATION

'Right here, right now is where we draw the line.' Greta's phrase sums up the desires of young people around the world, united in a great plan to heal the planet. That's enough now, they are saying, the time has come for the tide to turn. 'The moment for change has arrived. *Right here, right now.*'

Young people welcomed Greta's message and sent it round the globe, requoting these powerful words, posting them on social media, making them into hashtags and singing them at Fridays for Future, the demonstrations held every Friday since August 2018 in hundreds of cities. They have even danced to its rhythms in a remix by UK DJ Fatboy Slim, who took the most resonant phrase from

Greta's speech at the United Nations and superimposed it onto his classic dance track 'Right Here, Right Now'.

Appeals for action on climate change and constant reference to the consequences of changes documented by thirty years of science have given birth to a unique phenomenon. During her speech in Davos (at the World Economic Forum) on 25 January 2019, Greta Thunberg announced that 'our house is on fire'. Do you remember?

Our house is everyone's house. Our house is the Earth. This has become the rallying cry of a physical and conceptual entity to which we have given the simple name 'Green Nation'.

It is a state with no entry or exit barriers, in which people are united by a deep sense of responsibility towards the planet. It is an ecumenical nation, without political labels or ideological trappings but with one voice and one language, the universal language of science. The citizens of the Green Nation are millions of schoolchildren who think beyond geographical borders and do not see themselves as belonging to a specific country in the world but to something new and highly responsive, with no need for official declarations or stamped papers to justify its existence.

With the birth of this new phenomenon, Greta and her companions have demonstrated that you do not need to be an adult to understand what is going on in the world. They have shone a spotlight on a global collective identity, a shared sentiment that has forged a new language from irony and determination, communicated both through words and, crucially, through action.

The unwritten laws of the Green Nation include choices that young people make automatically nowadays, such as not wasting water, food, objects, raw materials and so on, small but vital changes in daily life which, if scaled up across the whole human race, could change the fate of this world. Reducing the use of plastic, one of the principal causes of pollution in our oceans, putting a bottle of water from home in your backpack to take to school, or when you go out, is now standard practice. Recycling is the norm, separating materials wherever you are, at home or out and about, whenever you can.

The Green Nation communicates through social networks and holds meetings in public spaces. Millions of children take to the streets and, without fear or awe, voice their anger at those who continue to disregard the evidence, the adults they are supposed to look up to (their families as well as government representatives). The Fridays for Future marches have always been peaceful and continue to be so, but this should not be interpreted as children waiting for the adults' permission to be heard. When an application submitted by a group of young environmentalists for a demonstration in London was turned down in October 2019, Greta said: 'If standing up against ... climate and ecological breakdown and for humanity is against the rules then the rules must be broken.'

In energy, consumption, transport, food – the whole economic system – change is here and the Green Nation has a big job on its hands.

THE GREEN NATION REVOLUTION

The aims of the Green Nation can be counted on the fingers of one hand. They are concise and essential. These hot-button topics are discussed and dissected by students on university campuses and in schools.

One: we have to stop burning fossil fuels, not in thirty years' time but right now, as an absolute political priority. If we don't, it will be impossible to keep a lid on the effects of climate change (according to the Intergovernmental Panel on Climate Change).

Two: we have to protect forests throughout the world and plant new trees, millions of trees. Only they can help us absorb the emissions already present in the atmosphere.

Three: we must be prepared to face the consequences of climate change, a preparation known to scientists as 'resilience', and help emerging economies to do the same.

Four: we have to promote equality. This means rethinking the way the Earth's resources, which are scarce and should belong to everyone, are used. Equality means promoting education, fighting world hunger and recovering land made uninhabitable or uncultivable through climate change or over-farming.

Five: we must reinvent the whole economic system. How, exactly? By finding new systems of production that do not exhaust our natural resources or pollute the biosphere, and finding new jobs that enrich society without impoverishing the ecosystem.

Essentially, nothing short of a revolution. **A Green Nation Revolution.**

CHAPTER 4

NEW ECONOMY, NEW NEW LIFE

FROM ETERNAL GROWTH TO THE CIRCULAR ECONOMY

Agatha is nine years old and makes small huts for her hamster out of old shoeboxes. She makes a rope from old gift-box ribbons, and transforms a shatterproof plastic beaker into a little elevator, inside which the hamster plays for hours. When the box reaches the end of its new life, Agatha cuts it up and uses the cardboard for other projects. She chooses to keep the huts she is especially fond of and puts the rest in the recycling bin.

Scaling this up (and exercising a little imagination), Agatha's room is just like our planet: a finite environment, or a 'closed system' as scientists describe it. Everything within these four walls is a source of play, work or inventiveness. Every material is used and reused several times, reimagined and adapted to the needs of the moment until, at the very end, it is returned to its source (via recycling) and reduced to its component elements, once again, taking new form and beginning a further useful life.

In her bedroom, Agatha has created a system she probably cannot name: the circular economy. Just what does this term mean?

When Greta took the powerful to task for deceiving the world with 'fairy tales of eternal growth', she meant just this: in a finite environment, like the Earth, eternal growth is a fantasy. In 1972, a team of researchers at the Massachusetts Institute of Technology (MIT) in the United States had stated the obvious in a report entitled *The Limits to Growth*. In essence, the report said that if the global economy continued production at a steady rate by extracting materials from the ground, transforming them and then throwing them away, within a closed system such as the biosphere, the result would be an impoverishment of the Earth's resources and an increase in global pollution.

The kind of economic growth we have become used to is known as linear growth and is based on the assumption that the resources at our disposal are infinite (because a line can extend indefinitely). The line in question is made up of three parts: extraction (of materials from the ground), production (of goods) and elimination (as waste).

However, the volume of fossil fuels (oil, gas, coal) available for extraction, for use in production and in transportation is anything but infinite. Indeed, many researchers argue that we have already passed the halfway point in the consumption of these resources that have been stored in the Earth for millions of years. The same is true of other materials, both mineral resources and others, such as aluminium (used for cans and in manufacturing many other things), iron and wood. And in the food-production chain, for example, there has been a collapse in fish stocks in our oceans.

So, what is the solution? Economic researchers have worked with geographers, social scientists and environmentalists to argue that a new economic model is required to slow this process of resource depletion and planet pollution. The new model is the circular economy: an economy that gives new life to materials and products, again and again, thereby mitigating the depletion of ecosystems and reducing harmful emissions.

According to research published by the Ellen MacArthur Foundation, we can eliminate greenhouse-gas emissions entirely by 2050 as long as we replace fossil fuels with renewable energy sources and if governments, businesses and ordinary people adopt the principles of the circular economy. We would also have to eat a sustainable diet (with minimal consumption of animal protein). These are the conditions needed to achieve the goal of limiting any increase in global temperature to 1.5 °C above pre-industrial levels by 2100. The Green Nation is wondering what we are waiting for.

THE CIRCULAR ECONOMY: A SUMMARY

What is the circular economy?

A system of economic development intended to benefit society, the environment and the economy itself. If these three systems worked together, they could provide mutual advantages without depleting the biosphere.

What are the fundamental aims of the circular economy?

- Reductions in energy waste, raw-material consumption and pollution.
- Maintaining products and materials over a cycle of use (reusing them multiple times).
- Regenerating natural systems, especially land, which is essential for food production and resilience (an area's ability to resist the negative effects linked to climate change).

What are business cycles?

There are essentially two cycles: **biological** and **technical.**

The **biological cycle** involves the production of food and other natural materials (such as wood or paper) that may be recovered to feed the manufacturing cycle through composting or anaerobic digestion (processes that create natural fertilizers). The ultimate outcome is improvement rather than exploitation of the Earth, the living system that originally gave rise to the production cycle. Regenerative agriculture makes use of this cycle.

The **technical cycle** makes use of technology (apps, for example) to recover and reform products, components and materials using the 'Four R' strategy: reuse, repair, reintroduce (into the production cycle) and recycle.

How can the circular economy reduce the volume of greenhouse gases in the atmosphere?

The circular economy extends the lifespan of products and materials, thereby reducing the amount of energy required to produce useful items and minimizing waste and pollution of the air, water and soil.

CIRCULAR ECONOMY SYSTEM DIAGRAM

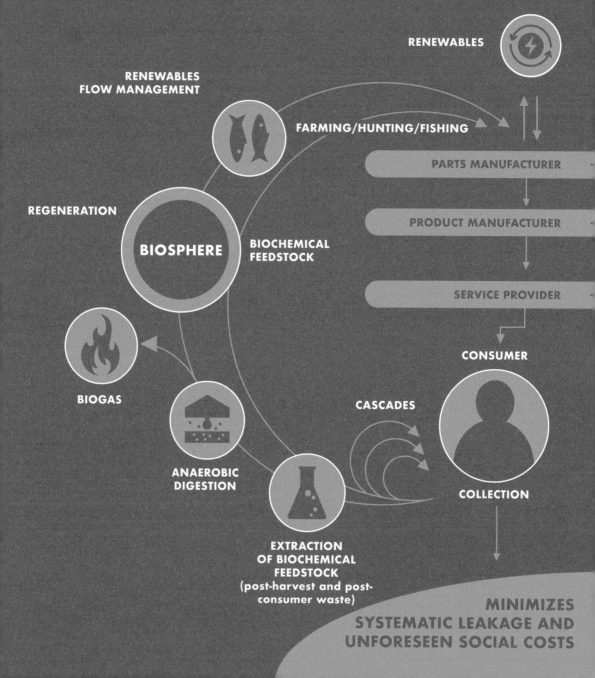

RENEWABLES

RENEWABLES
FLOW MANAGEMENT

FARMING/HUNTING/FISHING

PARTS MANUFACTURER

REGENERATION

PRODUCT MANUFACTURER

BIOSPHERE

BIOCHEMICAL
FEEDSTOCK

SERVICE PROVIDER

CONSUMER

BIOGAS

ANAEROBIC
DIGESTION

CASCADES

COLLECTION

EXTRACTION
OF BIOCHEMICAL
FEEDSTOCK
(post-harvest and post-
consumer waste)

MINIMIZES
SYSTEMATIC LEAKAGE AND
UNFORESEEN SOCIAL COSTS

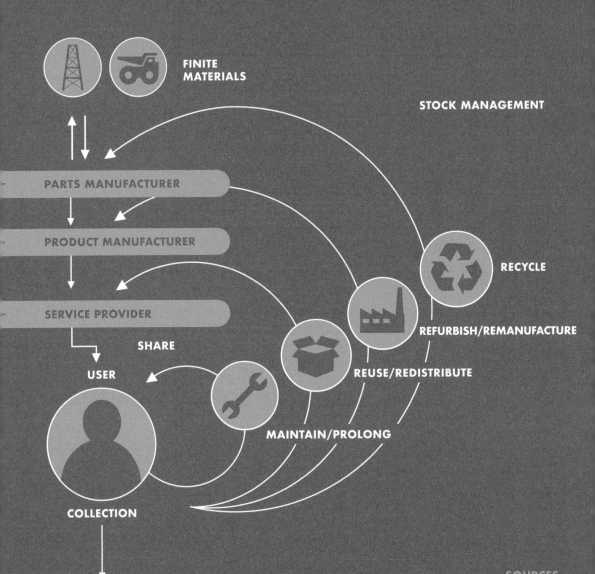

FINITE
MATERIALS

STOCK MANAGEMENT

PARTS MANUFACTURER

PRODUCT MANUFACTURER

SERVICE PROVIDER

RECYCLE

REFURBISH/REMANUFACTURE

SHARE

REUSE/REDISTRIBUTE

USER

MAINTAIN/PROLONG

COLLECTION

MINIMIZES
SYSTEMATIC LEAKAGE AND
UNFORESEEN SOCIAL COSTS

SOURCES
Ellen MacArthur Foundation
Diagram of circular economic systems
(February 2019)

Illustration based on
Braungart & McDonough,
Cradle to Cradle (C2C)

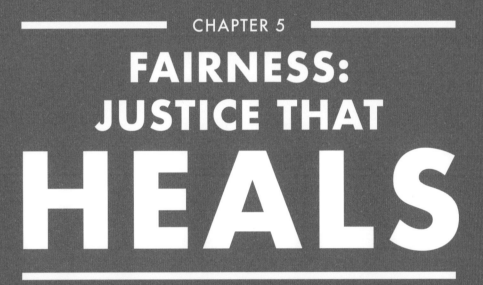

CHAPTER 5

FAIRNESS: JUSTICE THAT HEALS

FAIRNESS FOR
THE EARTH
AND ITS PEOPLE

Justice can be used as a tool in the fight against the effects of climate change, as demonstrated by the University of Cambridge, one of the first institutions to create a unit devoted to sustainability studies. It was brought up again by Pope Francis after he met Greta in the spring of 2019, and the pontiff returned to the subject at the United Nations (UN) in September of that year: 'The problem of climate change is related to issues of ethics, equity and social justice.... We are facing a "challenge of civilization" in favour of the common good.'

The concept of 'common good' also unites the children of the Green Nation. They do not strike or take to the streets for the interests of a particular individual but for all the inhabitants of our planet, this large and wonderful house of ours.

What do fairness and social justice really mean? Let's start with a fact: according to findings published by the UN bodies responsible for issues relating to the distribution of resources, such as food and water (the Food and Agriculture Organization or FAO) and the safeguarding of children's rights (the United Nations Children's Fund or UNICEF), the poorest populations will find themselves in the double bind caused by climate change *and* economic underdevelopment.

In Africa, for example, the main source of food and the principal livelihood of local inhabitants is agriculture, and 90 percent of crops are dependent on the volume of rainfall on the fields. This means that any change in rainfall cycles (or if precipitation is especially intense during the rainy season and completely absent during dry months) has a direct influence on the population of Africa's chances of survival. In addition, there is the immediate effect on the availability of drinking water caused by flood and drought: deluges contaminate wells and aridity dries them out, helping to spread serious epidemics.

Mozambique, where two-thirds of the population live in poverty, was struck by Cyclone Idai in March 2019, followed by Cyclone Kenneth only a month later. As many as one thousand people died in the subsequent flooding and three million were cut off completely and left to survive in extremely harsh conditions. Asia has proved similarly vulnerable: inhabitants of coastal areas in Bangladesh are abandoning homes that are routinely inundated and heading in their thousands to big cities that do not, for the moment at least, offer safe places to live nor employment for all.

The world's poorest populations are first to suffer the effects of such change, losing already scarce resources. Nations that have grown rich by consuming, and consequently polluting, much more and much earlier have a moral duty to treat this large portion of the world's population with fairness and justice. Such a strategy is also required to prevent an avalanche of negative consequences, including forced migration to places that are less affected and more resilient.

READY TO DRIVE CHANGE

Which levers could help achieve fairness? As part of its Agenda for Sustainable Development, the United Nations has for years provided the means to fight poverty, increase access to education and improve access to sources of drinking water or food. The problem is that these solutions are often helicoptered in from above (often for organizational reasons) rather than being the result of agencies listening to the needs of the local population and the policies they would introduce if they had the choice. **Listening takes time, and requires mediation and trained staff who can introduce innovations by adapting them to local conditions and cultures. It requires new plans and new professionals from throughout the world.**

At the same time, the multinationals that have exploited the resources of these countries for almost a century will have to rethink the way they operate in such areas in order to restore security, wealth and knowledge to the people who have always lived there. To achieve this, **the entire system of production will have to be modified and business development entrusted to those with a vision for the future of the entire planet and not just the immediate prospects of investors.**

Who has such a vision? The young people of the Green Nation are ready to usher in a revolution of the entire system based on data studies and scientific fact. Corporations and governments must devote economic resources in proportion to their wealth in order to support such new development processes.

CHAPTER 6

BUILDING
A BETTER WORLD
THROUGH
WORK

THE GREEN NATION'S
NEW JOBS

When I went to school, they asked me what I wanted to be when I grew up. I wrote down 'happy'. They told me I didn't understand the assignment, and I told them they didn't understand life.
John Lennon, musician

Could living in a sustainable city make us happier? If we could all drink clean water straight from the tap, without having to buy it in plastic bottles; read and write on 100 percent recycled paper; heat our homes with renewable energy sources; travel on public transport and electric bikes and make the air more breathable? A better world is not just for dreamers, as John Lennon once suggested: it is now a necessity. The most important jobs of the future are all directed towards sustainability; this dream is becoming a reality.

According to the World Resources Institute run by the World Economic Forum, 65 million new jobs devoted to conserving or caring for the environment could be created worldwide by 2030, both in traditional sectors such as manufacturing and in emerging markets such as renewable energies. Of the many new jobs to look out for, we have selected some of the key, well-paid specialist professions whose main requirements include competence, knowledge and empathy.

We do not need superheroes to save the planet; we need engineers, economists, scientists, biologists, environmentalists, architects and designers. We need young people who believe in the cause, who are able to see the world as it is and to imagine how it could be. The keys to success will be held by open-minded, curious and bold professionals, and start-up entrepreneurs who combine perseverance and imagination with the ability to reinvent day-to-day reality, just like Scott Munguía, a Mexican student who invented an entirely natural bioplastic by recycling the seed of the avocado, his country's national fruit. The main new professions will be:

Water-quality technicians. They will research creative solutions to water-related issues such as pollution and bacterial contamination. They will be chemists, biologists and graduates in environmental or earth sciences.
Recyclers. They will seek out every possible means to recover raw materials (principally paper, cardboard, aluminium, glass and plastic). Technology is changing the profession of integrated waste management with great speed.

Urban farmers. People are planting gardens on the rooftops of city buildings, combining two large sectors of green employment: food production (without pesticides or fossil fuels) and the green construction industry. These professions will include agronomists and students of regenerative agriculture.

Engineers. This ancient profession has now become more important than ever, especially in the design of systems to reduce consumption. Engineers are, for example, addressing the potential of renewable energy sources (sun, wind and moving water) and conducting studies into electric transport.

Environmental IT. Bio-informaticians and geo-informaticians are among the most sought-after professionals in the field of green employment. They deal with the services that involve energy consumption and work in the domestic automation sector (all the smart appliances in our homes that can be controlled remotely) and the IoT (Internet of Things), the invisible thread that connects such devices.

Sustainability architects. Architects are exploiting renewable energy sources in their urban, residential and environmental projects while recycling disused materials and limiting emissions at every stage of the process.

SUSTAINABILITY IS ALREADY IN FASHION

Did you know that sustainability has become such a major concern that many companies already have a dedicated sustainability manager? Claire Bergkamp, World Wide Sustainability and Innovation Director for the British fashion brand Stella McCartney (which joined forces with Burberry to launch the Fashion Industry Charter for Climate Action) was one of the first to take up this role, which involves studying production processes that respect the environment and promote social equity, from the raw-material production stage to distribution.

According to Claire, those wishing to pursue a career in the sector should make a choice between **environmental sustainability** (which addresses reductions in the environmental impact of the various stages in processing and the hunt for raw materials) and **social sustainability** (which ensures that human rights and employment rights are respected throughout the entire production process). The approaches to environmental and social sustainability are quite distinct and attract different people, with the latter appealing to more empathetic personalities and those who can understand and identify with life circumstances and working conditions that are very different from their own (in factories in developing countries, for example). This sensibility differs from that required to deal with sustainability from an environmental perspective or to make decisions about emissions or the sourcing of materials. There is a third field: **innovation**. As Claire explains, it is not just a matter of coming up with a new idea to conquer the markets or inventing the best running shoes: you must also ensure that you use biodegradable materials.

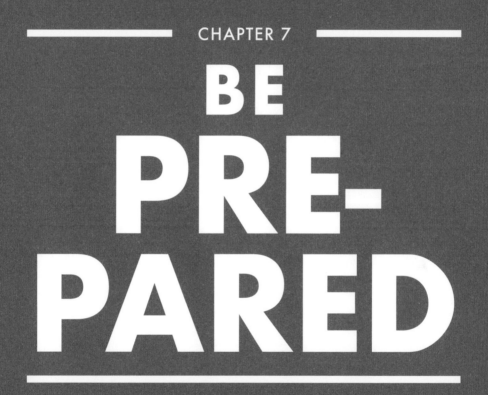

CHAPTER 7

BE PRE-PARED

STUDYING
FOR A BRILLIANT
GREEN CAREER

Young people still want to be astronauts or doctors, but, these days, the children of the Green Nation have more information at their fingertips and can see their future more clearly than those of earlier generations. At the heart of their ambition lies a very specific dream: to save the world. We have watched this dream come true in the creation of hundreds of new green jobs: high-tech creative and scientific careers that, according to the United States Bureau of Labor Statistics, 'produce goods or provide services that benefit the environment or conserve natural resources'. These professions will enjoy enormous growth over the next ten years.

There are many ways to prepare for a future that will combine personal ambition with an urgent need for positive change. New training courses and study programmes have already been created around the world and they are rapidly growing in number, taking the more traditional professions, from engineering to architecture and from science to economics, to the next level – the level of the Green Nation.

This transformation began in the university sector several years ago, when the most traditional faculties expanded their range of choices to include ecology-orientated courses such as Environmental Engineering for Sustainable Development or Mobility Engineering (training transport professionals). More specific courses have gradually been introduced by universities, including Ecological Economics, useful for an understanding of the value of natural resources and the environmental impact of companies' business activities. Environmental Science and Technology combines scientific and social subjects, examining pollution, for example, and the various strategies to reduce it. A three-year undergraduate course in Environmental Leadership trains socially responsible role models in the widest political and cultural contexts.

A total of 25 percent of the new undergraduate courses in STEM disciplines (science, technology, engineering and mathematics) introduced worldwide in 2019 are geared towards educating students to look for solutions for safeguarding the planet, bringing the problems associated with climate change and pollution to the test benches and experimental laboratories of the university sector.

Graduates in subjects with environmental specializations will have all the skills they need to work in the field of research and development, in start-ups (often founded by groups of university friends) and in all those illustrious companies that, in opening their doors to this new generation of professions for the first time, are facing up to pressing problems in need of a solution.

An education of this kind, based on solid scientific foundations with a healthy dash of creativity and motivation, will make all the difference to the young people of the Green Nation who are committed to their mission of saving the world. It is an attractive prospect for pupils about to choose their subject options. There is also the real possibility of progressing into exciting careers that are constantly developing. The findings of research centres suggest that it is precisely the jobs with links to sustainability that will grow both in number and in market value. These are dynamic professions that demand continuous expansion, in the form of fundamental research and experimentation, to find new solutions to implement.

It is vital, therefore, to have a strong academic background on which you can continue to build your specialist subject. A capacity for personal growth is essential and highly prized by entrepreneurs and backers of business ideas. Those who succeed in managing environmental issues while generating good results for the company itself, and the planet at large, will enjoy great success. By 2030, every business, both public and private, will be expected to come up with a robust and lasting response to climate change.

SIX GREEN UNIVERSITIES AROUND THE WORLD

NETHERLANDS, Wageningen University & Research This Dutch university offers two technical courses: **Soil, Water, Atmosphere** for those interested in working on environmental problems from a natural-sciences perspective, and **International Land and Water Management**, which combines engineering studies with social and natural sciences and addresses the drought, erosion and flooding that put food production at risk throughout the world.

FINLAND, Häme University of Applied Sciences (HAMK) For all those fascinated by Nordic design, this university has devised a course on ecologically and ethically produced intelligent design for small homewares, accessories and fashion items. There is a four-year degree in Culture and Art majoring in **Smart and Sustainable Design**.

ITALY, Polytechnic University of Milan Introduced in 2019, the master's programme in **Food Engineering** is for engineers whose job is to produce innovations across the value chain of the food and drinks industry's entire production, distribution and management processes.

SOUTH AFRICA, University of Johannesburg The aim of the undergraduate course in **Mineral Resource Management** is to train specialized managers in the mining sector with a view to gaining an understanding of resources and managing them effectively and safely.

USA, University of Minnesota The university's Institute on the Environment offers an interdisciplinary course that focuses on the study of **Ecological Economics**, reinforcing the relationship between natural resources and the environmental impact of the economy.

ARUBA, University of Aruba A specialist undergraduate programme in STEM disciplines (science, technology, engineering and mathematics) focusing on the sustainable development of small island states not unlike this Dutch island in the Caribbean.

CHAPTER 8

THINKING
BIG

NEW TECHNOLOGIES WILL
REVOLUTIONIZE THE PLANET

The plans instituted by governments to maintain global warming below +1.5°C are not fit for purpose and have a 50 percent chance of failing, as Greta reminded the United Nations: 'They also rely on my generation sucking hundreds of billions of tons of your CO_2 out of the air with technologies that barely exist.'

The technology currently available is not advanced enough to save the planet, but we have made huge progress over the last fifty years. Examples of this include the US Department of Energy's decision in the early 1970s to take a punt on something that, at the time, still seemed an impossible dream: turning sunlight into electricity. It was the time of the oil boom, when fossil fuels seemed to be the goose laying golden eggs for every economic growth plan; why bother to invest in an alternative? For the same reason that humans landed on the moon a few years previously: because we have always wanted to explore beyond the limit of our knowledge. And it was lucky we did, because what had seemed at the time an impossible feat is now a technology seeing constant growth, with installation costs that have dropped 80 percent, representing a true, cheaper alternative to fossil fuels. Solar energy has grown by 2,000 percent over the last decade, with China leading the field of the world's top producers (44 percent of global solar energy). While it is not enough on its own, this important breakthrough in the fight to reduce emissions and counter the rise in temperatures has been driven by technological innovation backed by both public and private research funding.

There are now other technologies to bet on, alongside renewable energy sources. Some are already in the implementation phase while others remain at an experimental level, with students at universities around the world looking for the best ways to apply them in daily life.

Intelligent and efficient storage-and-distribution systems (control centres, batteries for renewable energy) are at the cutting edge of research, as is the absorption of CO_2 from the air (although forests are the most effective in accomplishing this vital task for the sake of the entire ecosystem, as we have seen). Recycling of waste in general, and of non-biodegradable refuse such as plastics in particular, is of equal importance to researchers and investors alike. Another great challenge is to save energy linked to consumption, services and the manufacture of goods.

Young chemists and engineers are already launching revolutionary ideas onto the market, and their concepts only need further experimentation and a large-scale roll-out before making a real difference.

The information technology in everything that keeps us connected, from smartphones to computers, is one of the principal components of these ongoing revolutions. Start-ups all over the world are producing applications and specialized programs to manage the challenges and problems associated with the circular economy's new processes. Apps allow you to breathe new life into your jeans, for example, five or six times, passing them on through a points-exchange system to other users who are upcycling their wardrobe, before the clothes are finally recycled as simple fabric. Other apps help you track the sources of the food you buy at the supermarket, or allow farmers to monitor field irrigation so that no precious water is wasted.

A CRAZY IDEA (OR PERHAPS NOT?)

Among the most extreme technologies aimed at saving the planet come from the University of Cambridge and its Carbon Neutral Futures Initiatives department dedicated to studying as-yet-untested projects that could help us achieve net zero CO_2 emissions by 2030 (meaning that we absorb as much carbon dioxide as we emit). Three projects are explained below.

Refreezing the poles. The idea, whose feasibility is yet to be demonstrated, is to import millions of wind-powered pumps to the Arctic to spray salt water onto existing frozen surfaces to increase the thickness of the ice and counteract its melting. Costs amount to some US$500 billion but the main problems yet to be solved include the difficulty of constructing and transporting such a huge number of pumps, which would have to be made of stainless steel to withstand contact with salt water without deteriorating.

Recycling CO_2. This is a variation on the idea of capturing and trapping carbon dioxide, an idea that has been under investigation for years. The facilities in question (some of which are already being tested) are intended to absorb carbon dioxide from the atmosphere and to turn it into a new source of fuel using heat and a special process of chemical synthesis. The emissions created would restart the cycle, being captured in turn by plants in a kind of CO_2 recycling process.

Making the oceans greener. Algae can absorb CO_2 just as trees do, and some scientists have claimed that fertilizing algae in the oceans by introducing iron particles may trigger them to proliferate on the surface of the water, delivering an increase in the natural process of carbon-dioxide storage brought about by photosynthesis. This idea is not universally popular because it would make changes to marine habitats, but its proponents defend it with the time-honoured notion that 'desperate times call for desperate measures'.

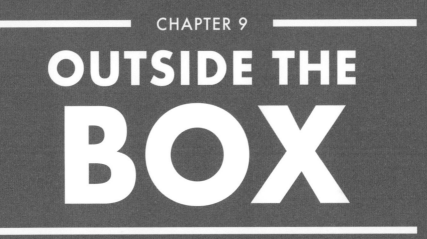

CHAPTER 9

OUTSIDE THE BOX

THE POWER
OF THE IMAGINATION

It took me four years to paint like Raphael, but a lifetime to paint like a child. **Pablo Picasso, the greatest artist of the 20th century**

How many times have you heard the expression 'outside the box'? Plenty, if you are part of the Green Nation generation. It means thinking about solving problems and situations by taking the road less travelled by those before you, breaking with conventions and expectations, and risking mistakes without fear of starting from scratch somewhere else, with another original idea. Outside the box is precisely where the Green Nation is looking for solutions to the problems arising from climate change, pollution and depletion of resources.

The work Greta has done, and continues to do, has played an important role in spreading the scientists' message to the widest possible audience and provoking a reaction from private citizens and governments. Scientists have been trying spread this message for more than forty years, but with only a few concrete results. Greta tore up the communications rulebook and, within just a few days, caught the attention of an untapped global audience through millions of online interactions. She has been a pioneer in the communication of scientific topics, and there are other young people just like her who have 'disrupted' the conventions in other sectors.

We see people making biodegradable plastic using bacteria that feed on waste; we see people building small devices that turn plastic bottles into construction materials to be transported to remote villages (thereby preventing non-biodegradable waste from mounting up on river banks or being washed into the ocean, as happens now). There are many others, some of whom we will meet in the next chapters.

There is an old saying that 'those who cannot remember the past are condemned to repeat it'. Young people do tend to ignore the way things have always been done and instead focus on what they must do next, but this is not necessarily a bad thing. In recent years, a great number of schools have begun to understand that encouraging individual perspectives on problem-solving, far from bearing out the old saying, can actually be a good way to prepare these young people for a future where uncertainty will require minds to be open and creative, and able to adapt quickly to change.

Young people today are prepared. They embrace unconventional ways of going about things and, across the globe, are introducing new approaches to the application of traditional sciences such as chemistry, biochemistry, engineering, biology and agriculture, and they are creating successful start-ups. The circular economy and zero waste are their guiding principles. The next stage is to source investments and apply their ideas to new businesses that will help solve a problem we must all own. Today's young people are creating a working future for the Green Nation, a future 'outside the box' that is resilient and successful.

NO ONE IS TOO SMALL

Our current priority is to save the planet from the damage caused by human activity over the past two centuries. Historically, young people have often been the ones to dream up inventions that have revolutionized life as we know it today.

The calculator. In 1642, at the age of just nineteen, Blaise Pascal, the son of a French tax collector, built the first automated calculator to help his father work on his accounts. It was the size of a shoebox and could add, subtract, multiply and divide using a series of gearwheels that were moved manually. It was dubbed a 'Pascaline'.

The television. In the early twentieth century Philo Farnsworth, the son of a farmer from Utah, had a passion for electronics (a science then in its infancy) and devoured magazines and anything else he could get his hands on in the local library. In 1920, at the age of fourteen, he was ploughing fields with his father when he had a stroke of genius. Looking down the parallel furrows left in the ground by the plough, he realized that if he could break down images into lots of parallel lines, find a way to transmit them electronically and then reassemble them at the other end of the wire, people would be able to see them as a whole on a screen. By the time he had turned fifteen, he had already put together a complete portfolio of scientific notes and structural diagrams to assemble the world's first television system. At the age of twenty-one, he managed to prove his theory by transmitting the first image. When he died, in 1971, televisions all over the world contained no fewer than 100 parts that he had patented during his lifetime.

CHAPTER 10

START IT
UP

INVESTING
IN GOOD IDEAS

Every year 1.3 billion tons of food are thrown away. This vast amount is equivalent in value to US$750 billion and could feed, four times over, the 821 million people affected by hunger across the world (Food and Agriculture Organization data from 2018). A total of 45 percent of this wasted food comes directly from our own homes: that inch of milk left in the bottle, the outer leaves of a lettuce, leftover pasta, overripe fruit. In 2015, Mette Lykke, a Danish businesswoman with a degree in political science who was keenly aware of the issue, found herself wondering how to get all this food back. Her idea was based on the economic principle of matching supply and demand. So, how did she plan to achieve her goal? By using a digital platform that connects those looking for a cheap meal (the demand) with those who would otherwise throw food in the bin (the supply), including restaurants and bars, canteens, supermarkets and bakeries. Too Good To Go was born as a London-based start-up that picked up 16 million Euros in various funding rounds (in which 'seed' capital is solicited from investors) and expanded rapidly in twelve countries, saving on average 20 million meals a year. Today, Mette manages a team of more than 400 young 'waste warriors' whose mission is 'inspiring and empowering consumers and businesses alike to take action against food waste'.

Mette's company is a concrete example of a successful start-up that bases its business firmly on the need to find solutions to the social and environmental issues that fascinate the young citizens of the Green Nation. Hundreds of young people like her have already launched their ideas into the world of sustainable business and, by taking the right steps, created thousands of new jobs with an ethical purpose, doing good both for people and the planet.

All these young companies, with their brilliant and positive ideas, must still attract funding, however. In start-up jargon, they need to be able to acquire the 'seeds' that allow the plant to blossom. Whoever provides these seeds (puts up the money) will have a fundamental role to play. 'A time will invariably come when it looks like everything is going to pot, when the business is not going to take off, and you start losing the faith you had in it before,' recalls Mette, 'and when that happens, you need investors who believe in you, who can show you trust and provide comfort.'

Recent years have seen the advent of business incubators to help grow these companies, often led by brilliant, young and still inexperienced entrepreneurs, as they are launched onto the market for the first time. Incubators are professional teams who take the founders of the most innovative start-ups in hand and help them negotiate a path through economic planning, financing and budgeting, tackling the complicated aspects of business in order to get their projects up and running. There are more than 7,500 of these worldwide, offering support, as well as things as basic as a desk or a physical space from which to network and meet other young people with all kinds of ideas awaiting realization, for an incubation period that may last from six months to three years. Tertiary education institutions are also keen to incubate the ideas of their own students and others.

According to the World Rankings of Business Incubators and Accelerators (a league table compiled by the Swedish organization Ubi Global, which has been rating the success of business incubators since 2013), the world's top tertiary-level incubator is called SETsquared and arose from an affiliation between the universities of Bath, Bristol, Exeter, Southampton and Surrey in the UK. The Polytechnic University of Turin's I3P programme in Italy has also been recognized as the world's top public-sector incubator, with 364 projects under management in 78 different countries in 2019 alone.

STARTING UP YOUR START-UP: FIVE STEPS FORWARD, ONE STEP BACK

Setting up your own start-up and making a success of it is a difficult, but not impossible, task. Here are some tips from start-up veterans who have made the grade.

1. Come up with an excellent idea. This is certainly a good place to start, but genius alone won't cut it: you need to turn it into a business idea and make it work on the market.

2. Analyze the market. In other words, ask yourself if your start-up will really help to improve people's lives.

3. Begin the search for the first 'seed'. Sourcing investments will require you to take part in as many funding calls (competitions) as possible and attend every event held to find new start-ups, including meetings with private companies. You will then need to get a pitch ready, a five-minute presentation in which the business idea is introduced.

4. Train the best team. Finding first the right partner or associate (who will be your co-founder) and then a group of people who have the skills to match your own vision is almost as important as the idea itself.

5. Strike while the iron is hot. According to a survey carried out by Bill Gross, the American entrepreneur who founded IdeaLab, being in the right place at the right time increases the chances of your start-up taking off by 42 percent. Now is the time to get started. It's a good moment for issues close to the Green Nation's heart.

6. Learn from mistakes. The innovator and investor Bob Dorf recommends that 'the first one or two thousand hours the founders dedicate to their creation should be spent pivoting: make improvements, rinse and repeat'. Many famous start-ups, from Twitter to Instagram, made it by learning from their setbacks and collecting feedback from customers and family members.

CHAPTER 11

TENDING THE
SOIL

REGENERATIVE AGRICULTURE:
A NEW WAY OF
FEEDING THE PLANET

A key term in economics is production, the process of transforming raw materials into a finished product ready for use or consumption. In the case of food (the basic product for human survival), agriculture and animal husbandry are the sectors that enable the transformation of fertile soil, water, plants and animals into the products needed to keep human beings alive.

To give you an idea of just how important they are, you need only remember that the agri-food sector in its broadest sense (including farming, forestry, animal husbandry and fishing) is the world's largest industry by size and turnover (by the number of people employed and the amount of money generated). There is one slight problem: according to a recent United Nations report, about a third of the cultivated land on our planet has been exhausted of its fertile capacity (its ability to transform a seed into an edible plant using solar energy, water and the nutrients in the soil). This is because the land has been so intensively farmed that it no longer has enough nutrients or energy for this process to be completed successfully. And, according to the United Nations again, if farming and cultivation methods are not radically changed, practically all other arable land will suffer the same depletion over the next sixty years. Moreover, emissions levels will continue to grow in lockstep with the global population and its need for food.

What does soil depletion mean? Let's make a comparison. Young people are potential producers of activity. In the morning, you get up, have breakfast and use the energy you have accumulated to go to school, attend lessons and study. You then take a break for lunch. After that you feel recharged and ready to face what the afternoon can throw at you, whether it involves a basketball game or a dance class. You relax in the evening after dinner before getting eight hours' sleep. By the morning, your body and mind have processed the nutrients you have taken in and regenerated themselves with rest; you are ready to face a new day and produce the same activity levels and the same results. Had you not eaten or rested, you would be in no state to do that.

In this respect, the land and the sea are not so very different from our bodies. They are living, vital systems with a capacity to transform individual elements into something of use to our bodies and those of the animals living on Earth.

Regenerative, organic and sustainable agriculture are methods that are continuously evolving in the search for answers to the most urgent questions: how can we nourish the soil without polluting it or depleting it with synthetic chemical fertilizers? How can we protect crops from pest attacks without poisoning the crops themselves? How can we capture carbon dioxide in the ground instead of watching it increase in the atmosphere as a result of greenhouse-gas emissions caused by farming or deforestation?

In addition to agri-food production, this entire value chain (harvesting, packaging and distribution) is an area of experimentation for increasing sustainability in the sector. Every stage that brings the product closer to our tables involves choices in terms of energy saving, emissions, conservation of the environment and protection of our forests. The new approaches available to the Green Nation, based on scientific studies into regeneration and increasingly inter-linked technologies have helped hundreds of new companies to flourish, with young entrepreneurs uniting in growing a better future. Agri-food, the largest economic sector in the world, is the new frontier for these pioneers, who are creating many sustainable jobs.

UNITED IN MAKING A DIFFERENCE

One of the most radical examples of regenerative agriculture comes from Yvon Chouinard, a rock climber, environmentalist and founder of the Patagonia sportswear brand. 'Regenerative agriculture can't be done on a large scale. It just can't. [The farmers we work with to grow organic and regenerative cotton in India] ... are getting rid of their bugs by squashing them with their fingers. ... Next year we've got 580 small farmers who will grow cotton this way.'

In fact, great progress in this sector has been made through the creation of networks that share knowledge and progress.

The United States, a country that has played a significant part in bringing about the environmental disaster, has seen the creation of Farmer's Footprint, a coalition of farmers, educators, doctors, scientists and entrepreneurs that records the human and environmental impact of chemical agriculture and suggests alternative approaches so that land can be cultivated cleanly. Its website contains many stories of small, trailblazing farming families who are making this ground-breaking transition. They have also issued an appeal: 'Over the last 40 years ... trends in farming practices have produced, for the first time in history, a nutrient-deprived, calorie-rich food system that has been scaled to feed the majority of the developed world. [This has resulted in] staple crops that lack the fundamental building blocks of biologic life, and are devoid of the medicinal components of those plants that have been the basis for healthy plants and animal/human consumers.' As consumers, fundamentally we need information so we can make educated choices about products that are good both for our bodies and for the planet. As the growers who have flocked to Farmer's Footprint have noted: 'It is time for the American consumer to empower our farmers to take back our food, and our right to the health that the food should bring us and our children.'

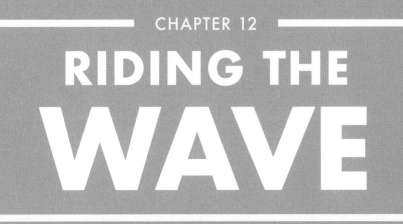

CHAPTER 12

RIDING THE
WAVE

THE FUTURE OF THE WORLD
IS WATER COLOURED

If climate change is the shark, then water is its teeth.
Paul Dickinson, CEO, Carbon Disclosure Project

The greatest impact of climate change has been on water and its availability, not only to human beings but to the biosphere as a whole. Melting ice sheets, disrupted ocean currents and increases in the severity and unpredictability of drought and flood have already had a significant, and visible, effect on our lives and those of all living beings. One of the most striking images to drive this concept home comes from the head of the Carbon Disclosure Project (CDP), a ten-year, international project to collect, process and study data on the CO_2 emissions of major industries and private companies around the world. Paul Dickinson, the CEO in question, noted: 'If climate change is the shark, then water is its teeth.' How can these terrifying teeth harm us? Given that water is the principal component of our bodies, of the animal kingdom and of the planet, it is easy to imagine how a change in the way our most vital substance behaves will have important consequences for our existence.

Drought and flood

According to Intergovernmental Panel on Climate Change scientists, it is now incontrovertible that 'human influences have affected the global water cycle and its patterns since 1960' and that droughts and flooding have intensified over the last sixty years. These extreme weather events have been responsible for the destruction of property through floods and for severe and sudden interruptions to the production of food, alongside disruption to the availability of drinking water for humans and animals. Such disasters can leave entire populations without food or water in a matter of hours, or contaminate the few remaining sources.

Melting of ice sheets and glaciers

Glaciers supply 50 percent of all the fresh water on the planet. As global temperatures continue to increase, the rate at which these precious resources are melting is rising – and they are failing to refreeze to the same degree. We are slowly and steadily losing our principal source of drinking water as the global population continues to grow.

If reducing emissions reduces global warming, and mitigates climate change, this also makes it the only way to 'shrink the shark'. A smaller shark will have smaller teeth, and so its bite may do us less harm. However, we will still have to try to contain the damage, the wounds caused by these bites, for the time being. And how do we achieve this? By trying to consume as little drinking water as possible for purposes not linked to staying alive, and finding ways to convert water that is not drinkable into water that is.

We can certainly all start doing this in our daily lives, but to make a difference on a grand scale, industry will have to change the way it produces and uses this precious resource. Here, new employment opportunities will arise for those tasked with the job of negotiating this important step in all sectors, from agriculture to industrial manufacturing.

The key terms in this new business are *water footprint* (based on the idea of carbon footprint, the recorded volume of emissions produced in creating goods and services) and *water purification*, the cleansing of polluted water, which includes the elimination of plastic and micro-plastics from the oceans.

THE ART THAT QUENCHES THIRST

We must work on ideas, projects and proven behavioural change to make a difference; combined, these three elements are extremely powerful and can transform the world. One such example is **One Drop**, launched in 2007 and based on an idea by **Guy Laliberté**, founder of the Cirque du Soleil entertainment troupe. One Drop provides access to safe water in so-called 'countries at risk', where there is no water or where fatal risks are attached to the water that is present. One Drop works by using art, a powerful lever, to raise awareness of concepts, from hygiene to the correct management of water resources, which improve access to this fundamental asset.

'Art is extremely powerful and can be used to change the world in a positive and impactful way. This was one of the initial ideas behind One Drop. We ... use art to ensure the sustainability of our water projects. Our approach also involves **Social Art for Behaviour Change**™ programmes and has received several world-renowned awards,' says Guy. This means creating a deep sense of involvement, awareness and responsibility in the communities in which the organization works. With its fundraising events that have involved many different artistic communities over the years, One Drop has raised and invested US$141 million in projects that will continue to improve living conditions for more than 1.6 million people in 13 countries across Africa, Asia and South America. The programmes help to realize the sustainable-development goals set out by the United Nations by guaranteeing the availability and sustainable management of water and sanitary resources for every country in the world by 2030.

CHAPTER 13

RECY-CLING

THE RALLYING CRY
OF THE GREEN NATION

Recycling is the bedrock of any strategy, process and economic sector aiming to face the challenges of emissions, pollution and resource depletion. Those who choose to invest in knowledge about new recycling and reuse systems, and how these are applied in working situations, are investing in the key aspect of the change that is the future of the Green Nation.

Let's take the recycling of an essential material like plastic, for example: as most of us know, it takes five centuries before its composite elements even begin to decay, during which time it will remain present in the ecosystem with consequences that we can as yet only imagine. According to the most recent projections, the oceans may contain more plastic than fish, by weight, by 2050. This state of affairs had become so shocking that in September 2019 the European Union and EuRic, the umbrella organization for Europe's recycling industries, signed the Circular Plastics Alliance's declaration whereby they undertake to recycle at least 10 million tons of plastic by 2025. The number may seem huge, but is dwarfed in comparison with the 8 million tons of plastic tipped into our oceans every year, the equivalent of a lorry load every minute. It's a good start, essentially, but there is still plenty to do. The companies and start-ups that will be able to help realize this aim, or indeed create a new way of dealing with plastic recycling, will be highly successful and enjoy sustained expansion with the creation and growth of new jobs.

In 2017, the Ellen MacArthur Foundation, which researches the circular economy, announced the New Plastics Economy Innovation Prize, an award for companies that come up with sustainable and entirely circular solutions to the problem of plastic, from manufacture to recycling. Packaging and its disposal are key features and companies are developing films and containers that appear to be made entirely of plastic but are, in fact, the result of processing plant-based raw materials (such as vegetation, wood or bacteria) alongside regenerated waste materials. With the required funding secured and the right manufacturing conditions in place, these businesses can expect to expand considerably in the future across a number of sectors.

Electronic gadgets represent a particularly promising area of recycling. According to a United Nations study, something like 42 million tons of electronic waste ends up in landfill every year, and this 'garbage' contains precious and highly recyclable materials such as copper, aluminium, titanium, gold and silver, not to mention glass, plastic and other metals. These all have great potential for reuse; in 2015, Apple alone claimed to have recovered nearly 1,000kg (2,200lbs) of gold (worth US$40 million) from its products in a single year. Recycling electronic waste correctly would result in a lower environmental impact and conservation of resources and energy (and a reduction in emissions). It would also bring an end to a trade in trash with the least developed countries in which millions of people, often children, work in precarious conditions. More than half of all such waste currently ends up following this route.

Investigating new recycling technologies and inventing new solutions and processes: these are the mantras of the Green Nation's economy.

THE WASTE ENGINE

Making use of recycled and discarded industrial materials is a way of life in Africa. People do it to survive, but also to create a new reality. **Kevin Kimwelle**, a young architect born in Kenya, has turned his ability to 'build from rubble' into an income stream that he finds satisfying and gratifying. 'At 18, I got on the bus out of Nairobi with a view to getting to know my country. I saw so much poverty, but also so much ingenuity. I fetched up in Port Elizabeth, a city in Nelson Mandela Bay with a population of 1.3 million people where 41 percent of families have no access to refuse-collection services.' Port Elizabeth is the capital of the South African automotive industry, however, and there are huge opportunities for recovering materials destined for the dump. Kevin's first project was a nursery school to the north of the city that was designed and built with the aid of the local community, 'a structure constructed entirely from recycled materials, including 2,500 glass bottles stacked up as a mosaic on the school walls, creating a magical atmosphere for the children'.

From landfill to the oceans to the big city, young, innovative companies transforming trash into treasure are now the most sought-after by public and private investors; their ideas and the passion with which they are realized always pay off.

The young engineers at **Recircula** in Barcelona have calculated that 34 percent of packaging produced in Europe every year is incinerated or thrown into landfill, incurring losses of 5.2 billion Euros. The principal reason for this waste is the lack of awareness among citizens about proper disposal of packaging. They have come up with a system known as Recysmart, a dumpster that recognizes packaging and a mobile app that interacts with local people; the key aspect of the project is to allow consumers to play an active role and to reward them with a series of incentives. Recircula aims to increase recycling of packaging by 15 percent.

CHAPTER 14
RENEWING
ENERGY

POWERING
THE FUTURE

Electricity enables the technology and digital devices we use every day to work. It really is what makes the world go round. It is also the power that helps us cool and heat our homes and is behind new forms of transport, from private cars to public vehicles that do not use oil, gas or petrol. But did you know where the name of this key modern force comes from? The answer is amber, a natural product known to the Ancient World. It was the Ancient Greeks (in about 600 BCE) who found out that the solidified, fossilized resin of certain trees possessed incredible properties: when rubbed, it emitted an invisible force that could repel or attract matter. And what did the Ancient Greeks call amber? *Elektron*. The name of the force that is the motor of our economy is derived from an old name for amber.

The rise in the use of fossil fuels in the twentieth century meant that there was enough energy to meet the electrical needs of industry, individuals and society in general, but it was the root cause of the subsequent increase in atmospheric emissions. A new and revolutionary concept has been making its way onto the market since the 1970s, however: renewability, or the potential to transform the energy produced by limitless sources, such as the heat of the sun or the power of the wind, into electricity.

These sources are now growing in importance and are key players in the sectors set to experience huge increases in investment and professional expansion. Let's take solar energy, for example. The US government's Department of Labor has estimated that the number of highly qualified technicians specializing in new photovoltaic systems (which capture sunlight and turn it into electricity) is set to double over the next six years, with growth in the number of employees and entrepreneurs in the sector due to exceed 100 percent in the United States alone. Growth in Europe and Asia is unlikely to be any less. These will be new types of professions, from planning and designing new light-capture systems (using next-generation photovoltaic cells) to the installation and repair of existing systems. The prospects for specialists in wind energy are similarly rosy; the number of professionals in this renewable energy sector, from engineers to technicians, to the people who maintain turbines, is set to double (at least) by 2026.

Other sources of renewable energy, alongside sun and wind, are witnessing a surge in employment opportunities as they help to save the world. These include hydroelectric energy and new ways (still at the experimental stage) of harvesting the power of ocean waves.

Designers will become vital in this sector. They can devise new systems for energy collection (photovoltaic roads, for example) and create networks between renewable sources such as those turning motion into electricity. In addition, we need storage for renewable electricity and distribution systems to take it to industry or consumers.

Renewable sources are not constant (the sun does not always shine, the wind does not blow at the same speed all the time), so storage is essential in order for it to be distributed when needed. The devices under closest scrutiny, by public and private institutions alike, include next-generation batteries, with investors in search of storage methods that maximize performance and minimize pollution. Scientists, chemists and engineers are the most sought-after professions for this task.

THE POWER OF THE ELEMENTS

Producing energy from renewable sources (and storing it) has become a mission for the bright young minds of Silicon Valley, the home of Apple, Facebook and Twitter, who are hoping to make their future cleaner and more efficient – and richer, why not?

The projects coming out of this corner of California, to the south of San Francisco, are an ingenious and innovative blend of long-term vision, cutting-edge technology, IT, artificial intelligence and sustainability. **Santanov Chaudhuri**, co-founder of the start-up **Hst Solar**, has developed a useful app to design large-scale solar-power plant projects, complete with layouts, maps and wiring loom designs to work out how many photovoltaic panels will be installed along a particular length of perimeter, enabling companies to reduce solar-electricity-generation costs by 30 percent.

The solutions identified in Europe for extracting energy from renewable sources are often more romantic, with a closer connection to the natural elements, but still as effective. With a group of very young mathematicians, Scottish aeronautical engineer **Simon Heyes** of **Kite Power Systems** has studied a system that obtains energy from kites. 'Ever since I was a child, I had enjoyed flying kites – I knew everything about them and had watched them for ages.' And then inspiration struck. They built installations, each consisting of a formation of kites equipped with advanced technology that hover about 450 metres (492 yards) above the ground, suspended in the sky and arcing in the power of the wind. Each pair of kites pulls on a cable that immediately rotates a turbine to generate electricity, creating a continuous source of energy. 'This system can be used on land and at sea; its strength lies in the potential of the kite itself, which can fly higher than a wind turbine and thus reach more powerful winds,' explains Simon. 'We believe that our system could be the magical solution to many of the world's energy problems. What's more, they are also very easy to carry around; all you have to do is fold them up.'

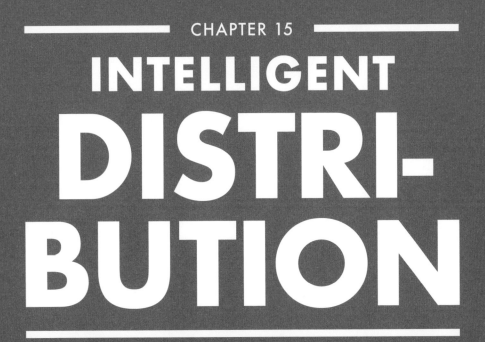

CHAPTER 15

INTELLIGENT DISTRI-BUTION

TRANSPORT THAT
POLLUTES LESS

Danny and Lydia usually go shopping on a Saturday or Sunday, buying everything they need for the week at the supermarket. They do not go out specially to visit the supermarket but usually drop in on the way back from an outing with their children or when running other errands. By contrast, 20-year-old Silvia, who is in charge of a research programme at a start-up, lives alone and never does a weekly supermarket shop, preferring to order items online a few at a time; if she runs out of something, she will go out in her car to buy it. Finally, Francesco, who travels only by bike or on foot, buys fruit and vegetables from a couple of farms not far from his home; he has chosen to use products that are available within short distances to satisfy his day-to-day requirements, and goes to the supermarket once a month to stock up on dry goods.

Alongside the habits adopted by Danny, Lydia, Silvia and Francesco, there are other kinds of consumer behaviour, all different in nature and in their carbon footprint. The distribution of products, and the supply of raw materials and the manufacture of finished products, is a fundamental element in any calculation of total emissions. According to recent research conducted by Walmart, the huge American wholesale distribution company, if a product's total emission is rated at 100, a good proportion of this (the percentage varies according to distance and transport choices) is emitted during what is known as the 'last mile', the journey it makes when transported from shop to home. But what does this mean?

Let's use a practical example from our new friends and a very familiar product: a pint of milk. If this pint is bought by Danny and Lydia along with twenty other products, as part of their weekly shop at the supermarket (where they have dropped in on the way back from some other errand), the milk's carbon footprint will be minimal, because the petrol or electricity used to transport it will be divided up between all the products purchased and the activities carried out (visiting grandma or an outing to a museum, for example). If the milk is bought on its own by Silvia, while dashing out to get supplies for breakfast, the final carbon footprint for the same pint of milk will be higher. Francesco's tally will be zero, however, because he will pick the milk up by bike, directly from the farmer.

Studying consumer behaviour and creating distribution networks that minimize their impact on the climate is as complex a task as it is important. Research bodies investigating large-scale distribution and e-commerce giants have been crunching complex numbers to try to make business more efficient and cleaner from the perspective of its environmental impact, not only over the last mile but also on the journey from manufacturing facilities to distribution centres (sales points or home delivery).

A key concept in these mechanisms is logistics. This term embraces shipping by sea, air or land, by road or rail (lorries or trains), the associated greenhouse-gas emissions arising from fuel consumption and general energy consumption. Another crucial consideration is packaging, with its double environmental cost: the energy required to produce the materials from which the packaging products are assembled, along with the pollution that such production processes can cause.

Logistically, the transport option with the lowest impact is by sea, but only if the container ships are efficiently loaded to maximum capacity and use the latest generation of fuels with low percentages of sulphur (mandatory from 1 January 2020 under a norm established by the International Maritime Organization). On land, the lowest impact comes from electric vehicles that get their power from renewable sources. In terms of packaging, the solution increasingly favoured by companies is to use wholly recyclable and biodegradable materials.

Many large firms have already integraged these choices into their sustainability mission statement and are actively sourcing and training managers who will work exclusively with this important part of their brand identity.

A BUZZ OF CHANGE

If the bee disappeared off the face of the Earth, man would have only four years left to live.
Albert Einstein, scientist

One of the many good things that bees help produce is packaging, and an idea with an Italian heart and mind (along with an entirely Californian approach to business) has been hatched to reward the hard work of the hive. The product, conceived in the intellectual space between San Francisco and Castelfranco Veneto (in the Italian province of Treviso), is a film of organic cotton that, when coated with beeswax, is leak-proof and can be shaped for use in packaging food, instead of plastic.

'The product is breathable, so it is perfect for bread, fruit and cheeses, for wrapping school snacks or to cover food leftovers,' say Massimo and Molly Massarotto, the creators and founders of **Apepak**. 'The film seals the wrap as the beeswax is activated by the heat of your hands. It is reusable (all you need to do is wash it out with a little water and vinegar) and it doesn't cause any pollution at the end of its life cycle.' The couple perfected the product over two years after 'roping in friends and relatives to test the product while working on research and development; more than two hundred families took part in experiments and filled out questionnaires; the California model has taught us to create a hypothesis, test it and modify it.'

Nature has always been a source of wonderful inventions: **Skipping Rocks Lab** is a London start-up that creates sustainable packaging from plants and seaweed. **Uwe D'Agnone** is a German inventor who has created paper produced from hay; you can even use the grass cuttings from any lawn.

The necessity of freeing the planet of plastic has indeed been the mother of invention, but we must also work on our lifestyles. The Green Nation is well aware that to change our destiny, we must first change our habits.

CHAPTER 16

FLYING
HIGH

TRAVEL THAT
ENRICHES EVERYONE

Sustainable travel is tourism that takes full account of its current and future economic, social and environmental impacts.
World Tourism Organization

Not everyone will be lucky enough to cross the Atlantic on a zero-emission catamaran, as Greta did from Sweden to New York (returning to Europe the same way, making landfall in Spain). Her decision not to fly was largely an act of principle, and a symbolic act to demonstrate that our habits must change, and quickly. We need to alter how we deal with transport and tourism, too. According to the European

Environment Agency, an aeroplane emits 285 grams of CO_2 per passenger mile, compared to just 14 grams for the same passenger mile of train travel, and zero grams for the same distance travelled at sea by a sailing boat equipped with solar panels.

Tourist travel is one of the large contributors to CO_2 emissions, with up to 5 percent of global emissions originating in this sector, which is still engaged in significant expansion. The number of journeys undertaken every year has doubled since 2000 (according to World Bank data) and international journeys alone now total 1.4 billion, according to the United Nations World Tourism Organization.

We need to undertake a number of short- and long-term actions to mitigate the impact of tourism. A key factor will be to rethink short-haul and medium-length journeys in a more efficient, less polluting way. Rail travel should be gradually shunted over to the latest generation of trains, for example, which use electricity from renewable energy sources. Developing technologies in air-transport options should result in electric or hybrid planes capable of travelling short distances, and research into low-emission fuels is underway for long-haul flights (these include options based on organic compounds or sourced from the absorption and recycling of CO_2). Research in this field is attracting the most brilliant minds, including young scientists and technical experts across the globe.

Other key aspects of sustainable tourism include preserving the natural environment, biodiversity and cultural heritage of the locations we visit. Going on holiday no longer means enjoying – and exploiting the wonders of an exotic place, leaving indelible footprints caused by emissions, pollution and the destruction of nature required to create locations fit to welcome tourists (everything from hotels to airports, for example). Tourism and the industry that surrounds it should instead become a way of bringing sustainable wealth and resources into an area that has chosen to invest in the conservation of its own habitat and the protection of a unique and fragile heritage.

Plenty of countries have already chosen to embrace the idea of zero emissions by building eco-resorts powered by renewable energy sources and applying the principles of the circular economy and the last mile in procuring goods and services. They also ask tourists to respect the area, its countryside and its traditions. Such undertakings require more careful planning than traditional resorts, however. Managers must be able to identify and implement sustainable hospitality policies, keep a close eye on outcomes and monitor the project's impact on the area and the environment, along with ensuring that visitors come away with great memories of the holiday. Positive experiences are most effective at changing habits, even in travellers.

INFORMED TRAVEL

There is no planet B. The Earth is our only home. The young citizens of the Green Nation know this only too well and are aware of how difficult it is to globetrot sustainably, however much they want to explore the world. Everyone involved in this enormous industry must participate.

Big hotel chains (Marriott, InterContinental and Hyatt) have finally eliminated single-shot bottles of soap and shampoo from rooms, replacing them with dispensers. This means that every year Hyatt removed 1.5 million bottles and Marriot saved about 2 million kilos of plastic. Innovative intercity travel start-ups include Germany's **Lilium GmbH**, a group of inventors with degrees in various disciplines (including robotics and aerospace engineering) at Munich's Technical University who are in the process of developing an electric jet as a kind of air-taxi service that you will be able to book with an app by 2025. The jet is emission-free and has an energy efficiency rating in line with that of an electric car, although you will be able to travel at up to 300 kilometres per hour (186 miles per hour): San Francisco to Palo Alto will take 15 minutes, Munich to Frankfurt an hour, tops. But what about the prices? Completely competitive, they say, when compared with traditional car-hire services.

In step with these ideas, political action is also becoming more effective, and the example of the Philippines, a country with one of the highest waste rates for plastic anywhere in the world, is highly instructive: the government, in the form of a courageous official from the Department of Tourism called **Bernadette Romulo-Puyat**, kept the island of Boracay (a tropical paradise that had been destroyed by pollution and an unsustainable influx of tourists) closed for six months. Once the damaged ecosystem had been repaired, Boracay was reopened and has now become a symbol for the informed rebirth of tourism.

CHAPTER 17

GREEN
BRICKS

BUILDING WITH ZERO EMISSIONS

Until a couple of years ago, a building had only to be constructed with a good standard of energy efficiency in order to be considered sustainable (in other words, designed to minimize the resources required to heat, light and clean it while causing as little pollution as possible). We now find ourselves asking if this was really the extent of the problem. How much does the *entire lifecycle* of a building affect its total CO_2 emissions, and contribute to climate change as a result?

Thanks to new ways of calculating the net cost (as developed by asso ciations of architects and builders from around the world concerned about sustainability), a building can begin to be truly green from the moment it is planned. The first question to answer is apparently simple: where should the building be built? Then come the next questions. How will it be connected with other buildings, with the services its inhabitants require, with transport infrastructure? How much will it cost to bring materials and supplies to the site? What kinds of materials are required to make it compatible with the local climate, to minimize the energy used to manage heat and cold in the relevant seasons? But, above all, can that same material be recycled and reused at the end of its lifecycle? How much pollution will we cause during the construction period, and what level of emissions will we produce? How can we offset all that?

Many calculations must be made and answers found that meet the needs both of the clients (those paying to have the building constructed) and the people due to live there. By making use of these calculations, we can save up to 50 percent of the total emissions for each building constructed or renovated (refurbishing is always the best option, to avoid waste) – an outcome for which it is worth concentrating the mind and devising new and brilliant ideas.

For this reason, design and construction professionals have had to go back to school in recent years in order to continue to do their work in a way that will be compatible with the principles of sustainability. It is no longer enough to plaster the roofs with solar panels or fill the walls with insulation to reduce heat loss.

Now, professionals need to understand how to reduce what is known as embodied carbon (the emissions of carbon dioxide intrinsic to the construction process itself) rather than just the operational carbon (the emissions caused by energy consumption arising from use of the building – switching on lights, heating, operating the drainage system, and so on). Young people now graduating from university and technical schools will already have spent several years addressing these problems in courses examining sustainable architecture. Most importantly, they have the open-mindedness and sensitivity required to incorporate all these variables into projects that nurture the green shoots of change for the Green Nation.

And speaking of green shoots, we must not forget the plants. Do you remember how much carbon dioxide they can absorb from the atmosphere? Green architecture has for some years now been introducing the concept of plant walls, walls covered in vegetation, and plenty of architects have already taken this on board; recent projects are moving at a faster pace on the sustainability of maintaining such vertical forests. Irrigating and fertilizing such structures is not an easy task, often incurring energy waste and requiring the use of substances with high emission rates. The challenge now is to make them completely autonomous, to integrate them as completely as possible into their surroundings and keep them going with natural elements instead. This challenge will demand fresh ideas and new professionals to implement them, so that eventually entire cities can be covered with greenery.

SMART CITIES

The sustainability of any architectural project (building using components and materials that can be easily recovered, reused and scrapped without polluting) has become an essential aspect of our way of life.

As part of the most recent Climate Action Summit in New York, Stefano Boeri, an internationally renowned architect, presented **Smart Forest City**, a self-sufficient and entirely sustainable urban project that is to take shape in Mexico over the next few years. The world's first smart green city is set to be created on a 560 hectare site featuring roads equipped with recharging systems for electric vehicles and drones that will be used to fetch supplies. There will also be a vast amount of greenery, both on the streets and in the houses, as it becomes an integral aspect of the city.

Making the world a better place by redefining the concepts of 'the city' and 'the home' will take both imagination and effort. **Sustainer Homes**, a start-up founded several years ago by Gert van Vugt, a former student at Utrecht's University College in the Netherlands, has begun construction of self-contained, relocatable shipping-container houses that can provide affordable and sustainable housing. Each unit uses electricity generated by solar panels and wind turbines that guarantee a year-round supply of energy. A highly efficient heat pump combined with top-quality insulation ensures that every home is warm in winter and cool in summer. Water is collected from the roof and filtered for safe human consumption; once used, it is then passed through a plant-based filter and returned to the ground. All the construction materials are reusable and recyclable.

'If we want to live sustainably alongside 10 billion other people, we will have to reinvent the way we construct our buildings,' says the start-up's founder. 'We will look back at the current way of building and think: why didn't we do it sooner?'

CHAPTER 18

REINVENTING
FASHION

STYLE WITHOUT CONSEQUENCES

Buy less. Choose well. Make it last. Quality, not quantity. Everybody's buying far too many clothes.
Vivienne Westwood, British fashion designer

Making a single pair of jeans consumes 7,500 litres of water, equivalent in volume to the average amount each of us has drunk over the last seven years. This figure is so incredible it seems impossible. We are used to thinking that other sectors have the greatest impact on climate change and the consumption of natural resources, but the fashion industry is single-handedly responsible for almost 10 percent of our total emission of greenhouse gases, more than all transport by air and sea combined. This was announced by the UN Alliance for Sustainable

Fashion, a new United Nations organization created at the end of 2019 to monitor the impact of the sector and to work with scientists and industrialists to find solutions compatible with the Agenda for Sustainable Development and reduction of greenhouse-gas emissions. It is an urgent issue because continuing with business as usual could mean a rise in industrial output by as much as 50 percent by 2030.

According to their data, the fashion industry uses 93 billion cubic metres of drinking water every year, equivalent to the annual requirements of five million people. The processes required (fabric and leather dyeing, in particular) result in by-products that account for 20 percent of global water pollution, not to mention the half a million tons of microfibres that are dumped into the oceans on an annual basis. A real problem, in other words.

The problem blew up twenty years ago, when the fast-fashion market (delivering a new collection every few weeks) took off on a global scale; a truckload of clothes or accessories is now carted off to the dump every second. The big brands and major distributors are already rejigging their business models to integrate the principles of sustainability, both in terms of global emissions and pollution in general.

While giants such as H&M, Zara and Gap are blazing a trail with investments in research and training programmes for staff specializing in dealing with such challenges, there are myriads of small and medium-sized enterprises all over the world that will need to share inventions, solutions and guidelines if we want a satisfactory global outcome. We may think that these giants dominate the market, but production is, in fact, highly fragmented. The four big names in China that churn out fast fashion for other brands account for only 5 percent of total production, for example; a considerable effort of communication and persuasion will be required on the part of both industry and governments to lead all the other entrepreneurs (in China, the remaining 95 percent!) down a sustainable path.

But what will these solutions be? We need a plan that will combine a range of different interventions, the first of which will be a drastic reduction in fossil-fuel use in favour of renewable sources in a product's lifecycle – coal is still the main energy source for micro-producers in India and other Asian countries. Second, we need to create dyeing processes that use less water and do not dump toxic elements into the environment. Third, we need to apply the principles of the circular economy in order to recycle raw materials and thus reduce costs (arising from emissions). Regenerative agriculture will once again be a key consideration; if the recycling of natural fibres such as cotton could be complemented with new methods for growing plants, helping them to trap CO_2 and feeding the soil rather than depleting it, for example, the picture would be complete.

Fashion is just one of the industries in which there is great opportunity to work at different levels towards sustainable goals. And let's not forget the creative approach: finding ways to breathe new life into used materials is as important as coming up with a new technique to dye a fabric or produce it in the first place. There are literally hundreds of possibilities that the young people of the Green Nation will have to deal with.

NEW ANTI-WASTE TRENDS

The date 24 August 2019 was important in the annals of the fashion industry, marking the debut of Fashion Pact, an agreement among the main fashion brands committing them to taking effective action in the fight against climate change. Signatories included Gucci, Chanel, Hermès, Stella McCartney, H&M, Farfetch, Calzedonia and Nike, with a total of 56 firms involved representing 250 international brands. It was not simply an altruistic act; these companies have cottoned on to the fact that the young people of the Green Nation are informed in their shopping. An awareness now underlies the purchase of new trainers, a new fleece or hoodie, or even a football or basketball, redefining the way we consume fashion.

Vivienne Westwood, environmentalist and doyenne of punk, was ahead of her time ten years ago when she chose a microstructure of young people from Nairobi to produce the Handmade with Love bag that has since become an icon of ethical fashion. The same Kenyan firm has been providing the brand with a range of high-end accessories made from recycled canvas and cotton, or unused scraps of leather or paper, since 2015. A sustainable alternative has thus been developed to create wealth in developing parts of the world, permitting local workers to pass on their skills to future generations.

By integrating ethics and aesthetics, working on responsible innovation and using new technologies, sustainability is rewriting the rules of the game. The scientists at London's **Worn Again Technologies** have spent six years working out what to do with fabrics that are no longer usable. 'There was a need to turn old things into new,' say the company's founders. 'Our technology sorts and decontaminates waste fabrics, bottles and PET packaging before extracting the polyester polymers and cotton cellulose and transforming them into new raw textiles that are also competitive from an economic perspective.' A stroke of genius, don't you agree?

GLOSSARY

Agrifood chain: harvesting, packaging and distribution; the process that brings food products from their source to the consumer.

Biosphere: all living organisms.

Business incubators: universities and companies that help start-ups take their first steps onto the market.

Carbon footprint: the total volume of emissions produced to create particular goods or services.

Circular economy: a developmental system designed to benefit society, the environment and the economy itself. It aims to reduce pollution and wastage of raw materials by reusing resources to make new products. No waste leaves the circle.

Ecosystem: the interaction of organisms with each other and their surrounding environment.

Embodied and operational carbon: the former is the total volume of carbon dioxide emissions inherent in the construction of a building, while the latter is the volume of emissions arising from the energy consumption occasioned by the building's use.

Energy efficiency: the ability to bring about a result using less energy than other systems.

Equity and social justice: useful tools to fight poverty, lack of education and limited access to supply lines (food and water).

Fast fashion: lines and collections with a short shelf-life and very high levels of waste.

Fossil fuels: oil, coal and natural gas, created through the transformation of organic substances laid down in the ground millions of years ago. When burned, they produce energy and carbon dioxide.

FridaysforFuture: a global student movement established in 270 countries at the end of 2018 with the aim of drawing the attention of governments and society at large to the effects of climate change. The movement grew up around the message from Greta Thunberg, a young Swedish activist.

Green Nation: a virtual and symbolic nation of millions of young people who are united by a deep sense of responsibility towards the planet. A nation without boundaries, without political labels or ideological affinities, and speaking one common language – that of science.

Last mile: the journey goods make from store to the purchaser's home, often the major source of that product's carbon footprint.

Outside the box: blue-sky thinking, finding novel solutions.

Regenerative agriculture: a farming method that makes use of the generative capacity of land without depleting it while also avoiding the use of synthetic chemical fertilizers.

Start-up: a new company propelled by brilliant and positive ideas.

Zero emissions: production of energy that does not involve the emission of greenhouse gases, including CO_2.

Zero waste: a cyclical refuse-management strategy that transforms waste products into resources that can be reused.

BIBLIOGRAPHY

Special Report on Global Warming of 1.5 °C, Intergovernmental Panel on Climate Change (IPCC), October 2018.

The Sustainable Development Goals Report 2018, United Nations, New York, 2018.

Completing the Picture: How the Circular Economy Tackles Climate Change, Ellen MacArthur Foundation, 2019.

World Employment Social Outlook: Trends 2018, International Labour Office (ILO), Geneva, 2018.

The State of Food Security and Nutrition in the World 2018. Building Climate Resilience for Food Security and Nutrition, Food and Agriculture Organization (FAO), Rome, 2018.

Transport-related CO_2 Emissions of the Tourism Sector, World Tourism Organization, 2019.

WEBSITES

www.cdp.net
www.eea.europa.eu
www.ellenmacarthurfoundation.org
www.energy.cam.ac.uk
www.euric-aisbl.eu
www.fao.org
www.farmersfootprint.us
www.fridaysforfuture.org
www.futurecoalition.org

www.ipcc.ch
www.onedrop.org
www.schoolstrike4climate.com
www.ukscn.org
www.unfashionalliance.org
www.unfccc.int
www.unicef.org
www.unwto.org
www.weforum.org

ACKNOWLEDGEMENTS

Thank you to Balthazar Pagani and Manuela Marazzi for helping to cultivate the new shoots of the Green Nation in bookshops all over the world.

Our thanks go out to Constant Tedder and all the team at The Hive Spring, Hong Kong, for assisting at the birth of this book in a beautiful and sustainable co-working space.

Thank you to all the mothers and fathers who helped us find out what we had to know to support the children in choosing a green future.

Thank you, Salvatore Giannella and Manuela Cuoghi.

Thanks also to Gianni, Alessandro and Giovanni, and to Massimo. And to Agata and Leonardo, our first readers, aged between nine and forty-five.